Eve of 1

News for every day of the year

Marilyn Monroe entertains US troops in
Korea, 17 February 1954.

By Hugh Morrison

MONTPELIER PUBLISHING

Front cover (clockwise from left): Elvis Presley records his first song on 4 January. The Castle Bravo atom bomb test takes place on 1 March. Marilyn Monroe entertains the US army in Korea on 14 February. Roger Bannister runs the four minute mile on 6 May. The world's first transistor pocket radio is launched on 18 October.

Back cover (clockwise from top): Marlon Brando stars in *On The Waterfront*, released on 28 July. Janet Leigh stars in *Living It Up*, released on 23 July. Maureen Connolly (USA) wins the French Open tennis championships on 29 May. William Golding's novel *Lord of the Flies* is published on 17 September. The Iwo Jima Memorial is dedicated on 10 November. HM Queen Elizabeth II and HRH Prince Philip begin their Australian tour on 3 February.

Image credits: Drew Crawford, Airwolfhound, Henri Manuel, Glenn Francis, Gabott, Allan Warren, Alan Light, Michael Pitcairn, Joe Haupt.

Published in Great Britain by Montpelier Publishing.
This edition © 2023. All rights reserved.
www.hughmorrisonbooks.com

ISBN: 9798860535312

January 1954

Friday 1: The first nationwide colour TV broadcast is made in the USA.

Kingsley Amis' comic novel *Lucky Jim* is published.

Saturday 2: The French army reports a major buildup of Vietminh communist rebel forces surrounding the last French stronghold in Vietnam at Dien Bien Phu.

Sunday 3: Television broadcasting begins in Italy.

Elvis Presley makes his first record on 4 January.

The last steam passenger train service ends in the USA, between Washington DC and Richmond, Virginia.

Monday 4: Elvis Presley makes his first demo recording for Sun Records in Memphis, Tennessee.

Tuesday 5: US socialist campaigner Countess Dorothy Di Frasso dies aged 65 of a heart attack on a train near Las Vegas, Nevada.

Wednesday 6: 16 people are killed when an RAF Vickers Valetta T3 training aircraft crashes near Albury, Hertfordshire.

January 1954

Thursday 7: The first demonstration of a computerised translation system (Russian to English) takes place using an IBM computer in New York City.

Friday 8: The government of India makes a formal complaint to North Korea due to the slow release of Indian Army troops taken prisoner during the Korean War, which ended in 1953.

RKO Studios is fined $25,000 for releasing the film *French Line,* starring Jane Russell, without certification by the Hays Code board of censorship. The film is also banned by the Catholic League of Decency, and Jane Russell herself refuses to attend the premiere.

Jane Russell is caught up in controversy on 8 January

Saturday 9: Violent clashes are reported to have been raging for 48 hours around the French outpost of Donghene, one of the last footholds of French colonial authority in Indochina (now Vietnam).

A 1950s IBM computer in operation. On 7 January the first translation program is launched using a computer of this type.

January 1954

Above: Marilyn Monroe and Joe DiMaggio are married on 14 January.

Sunday 10: 35 die when a deHavilland Comet jet liner, BOAC Flight 781 disintegrates in mid-air due to metal fatigue over the Mediterranean near Elba.

Monday 11: Viscount Simon, one of only three British politicians to have served as Home Secretary, Foreign Secretary and Chancellor of the Exchequer, dies aged 80.

Tuesday 12: 125 people are killed in an avalanche in the village of Blons, Austria.

Wednesday 13: The US Secretary of State John Foster Dulles warns that re-uniting North and South Korea may be impossible because communist China is 'gobbling up' the north into a de facto province.

Thursday 14: Hollywood star Marilyn Monroe marries the baseball player Joe DiMaggio.

Friday 15: Waruhiu Itote, leader of the Mau Mau resistance against British rule in Kenya, is captured.

Saturday 16: The Rodgers and Hammerstein musical *South Pacific* closes on Broadway after 1,928 performances.

Sunday 17: Soviet leaders begin a purge in Georgia, with police leader Vilian Zodelava executed for treason.

Sidney Greenstreet dies on 18 January.

January 1954

The USS *Nautilus* is launched on 21 January.

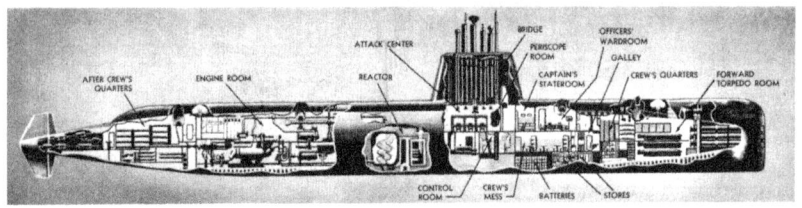

Monday 18: Actor Sydney Greenstreet (*The Maltese Falcon*) dies aged 74.

Tuesday 19: The Indian Army announces the release of 22,000 prisoners of war held captive in North Korea since 1953.

Wednesday 20: The Maranouchi Line, Tokyo's second underground railway line, is opened.

Thursday 21: The world's first nuclear-powered submarine, the USS *Nautilus*, is launched by America's First Lady, Mamie Eisenhower.

Friday 22: The Biblical epic *The Robe*, starring Richard Burton and Jean Simmons, is awarded 'Best Picture' in the 11th Golden Globe Awards.

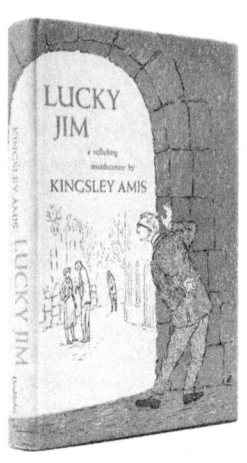

Kingsley Amis' first novel, *Lucky Jim*, is published on 1 January.

January 1954

Saturday 23: British, American and French representatives gather in Berlin for talks with the Soviets on the war in Indochina.

Sunday 24: The USSR's representative in the Berlin peace talks, Vyacheslav Molotov, demands that China be admitted to the discussion; the idea is rejected by other attendees.

Monday 25: Dylan Thomas' radio play *Under Milk Wood,* starring Richard Burton, is broadcast for the first time.

Richard Burton stars in *The Robe*, awarded a Golden Globe on 22 January.

The writer Ernest Hemingway and his wife are rescued three days after their plane crashes in northwest Uganda.

Tuesday 26: 5000 Red Chinese soldiers defect to Nationalist forces in Taiwan under Chiang Kai Shek.

Madrid Radio is seized briefly by militant students demanding the return of the British colony of Gibraltar to Spanish rule.

Wednesday 27: 21 American, 1 British and 325 South Korean prisoners of war state they wish to remain living in North Korea after their release following the Korean War; Allied spokesmen claim they may been 'brainwashed'.

Archie Moore beats Joey Maxim to retain the World Light Heavyweight boxing title at the Orange Bowl, Miami.

Thursday 28: The Berlin peace talks stall after the Soviet demands to include communist China are formally rejected by the western Allies.

Archie Moore.

January 1954

Friday 29: Martial law is declared in Syria by President Adib Shishakly after an attempted coup.

The talk show host and author Oprah Winfrey is born in Kosciusko, Mississippi.

Saturday 30: 22 former Gestapo agents are sentenced to death in a military tribunal held in Marseille, France.

Sunday 31: As the French hold on Indochina weakens, colonial troops from 38 outposts desert to join the communist Vietminh rebels.

Oprah Winfrey is born on 29 January.

A French soldier on patrol in Indochina. Large-scale desertions by colonial troops take place on 31 January.

February 1954

Monday 1: The Berlin peace talks stall as the Soviet delegation insists on a reunified Germany only if Soviets are installed in key government positions.

Royal decorations in Brisbane are erected for the Queen's visit to Australia on 3 February.

Tuesday 2: The US government announces 500 air force technicians will be sent to advise French forces in Indochina; it is one of the first steps towards American military involvement in Vietnam.

Wednesday 3: HM Queen Elizabeth II becomes the first reigning monarch to visit Australia.

Thursday 4: 300 people are killed in a stampede during at the Kumbh Mela religious ceremony by the River Ganges near Benares, India.

Friday 5: The Soviet Union offers Britain £400m worth of

February 1954

Above: *I Love Lucy*, starring Lucille Ball and Desi Arnaz and *Dragnet* starring Jack Webb (below) top the bill at the Emmy Awards on 11 February.

industrial contracts in a bid to improve east-west relations.

Saturday 6: The former US President Harry S Truman calls the investigation into communists in public office by Senator Joseph McCarthy as 'one of the biggest ever hoaxes attempted in American history'.

Sunday 7: Hundreds of people are arrested following pro-democracy demonstrations across Soviet controlled East Germany.

Monday 8: Silent film star Laurence Trimble dies aged 68.

Norwegian police announce the breakup of a Soviet spy ring operating near NATO offices in Oslo.

Tuesday 9: French colonial forces announce that Vietminh rebels are surrounding the Laotian capital, Luang Prabang.

Wednesday 10: Britain's Jean Westwood and Lawrence Demmy win the Ice Dancing category at the World Figure Skating Championships in Oslo, Norway.

Thursday 11: *I Love Lucy* wins Best Comedy and *Dragnet* wins Best Mystery Program at the 6th Emmy Awards ceremony in the Hollywood Palladium, Los Angeles.

Friday 12: French heavy bombers attack 10,000 Vietminh ground troops surrounding the Laotian capital of Luang Prabang.

February 1954

Saturday 13: In the Berlin peace talks, the Soviets refuse to withdraw their troops from Austria, occupied since 1945. The Soviets finally leave in October 1955.

Sunday 14: French colonial troops engage with Vietminh communist forces in pitched battles around the Laotian capital, Luang Prabang, as the communists close in.

Monday 15: The cartoonist Matt Groening, creator of *The Simpsons*, is born in Portland, Oregon.

Vietminh forces in Indochina. The Vietminh clash with French troops in Laos on 14 February.

Tuesday 16: A 24 hour general strike takes place in Rome in protest against the government of Mario Scelba.

Wednesday 17: French colonial forces report a massacre of 1400 Catholic civilians in Thang Thuoung, near Hanoi, Indochina, by Vietminh communist rebels.

Thursday 18: Actor John Travolta (*Saturday Night Fever*) is born in Englewood, New Jersey.

John Travolta is born on 18 February.

Friday 19: The Soviet Union transfers control of the Crimea from Russia to the Ukraine.

Facundo Bacardi, 8, heir to the Bacardi rum fortune, is kidnapped and held for ransom in Havana, Cuba. He is released unharmed when police shoot dead one of his captors.

February 1954

Liberace causes a riot on 20 February.

Saturday 20: Police in Miami, Florida, struggle to control a crowd of 10,000 people, mostly women, attending an opening of a bank by flamboyant celebrity pianist, Liberace; several women faint and some receive minor injuries in the crush.

The government of South Korea proposes an anti-communist alliance with the kingdoms of Laos, Cambodia and Vietnam.

Sunday 21: Star Trek actor Leonard Nimoy marries actress Sandra Zober.

Monday 22: It is announced that TRH Prince Charles and Princess Anne will join their parents HM Queen Elizabeth II and the Duke of Edinburgh on the final leg of their royal world tour of on 15 April. The Queen is reported to be missing her children greatly since starting the tour in November 1953.

HM Queen Elizabeth II and the Duke of Edinburgh on the royal tour of Australia. On 22 February it is announced their children will join the tour.

February 1954

Tuesday 23: The first mass vaccination of children against polio begins, in Pittsburgh, Pennsylvania.

Wednesday 24: French colonial forces in Indochina report that Vietminh rebel forces have halted their advance on the Laotian capital, Luang Prabang.

Thursday 25: Gamal Abdel Nasser becomes Prime Minister of Egypt.

A second coup attempt in Syria is successful as President Adib Shishakli is ousted by a military junta.

Gamal Nasser becomes Egyptian PM on 25 February.

Friday 26: Recep Erdogan, President of Turkey, is born in Istanbul.

Reverend William Inge, theologian and Dean of St Paul's Cathedral, London, dies aged 93.

Saturday 27: The British government announces it will resume trading with Poland and Hungary; economic relations were broken off in 1949 following political disputes.

Sunday 28: Troops fire on demonstrators in Syria unsatisfied with the resignation of President Shishakli on 25 February; they demand an entirely new government.

March
1954

Monday 1: Four Puerto Rican nationalists open fire in the US House of Representatives, wounding several congressmen; they are all apprehended and serve 34 years in prison.

Castle Bravo, a 15-megaton hydrogen bomb is exploded by the Americans on Bikini Atoll.

US Evangelist Billy Graham begins his three month 'London Crusade' of religious rallies, reaching up to three million people.

Tuesday 2: Vietminh rebels in colonial Indochina divert their forces from the capital, advancing to within a mile of the last major French stronghold at Dien Bien Phu.

Wednesday 3: 29 people are killed when a Turkish State Airlines plane explodes shortly after takeoff from Adana, Turkey.

Thursday 4: The United Nations announces new disarmament talks for the US and USS'.

Friday 5: The musical comedy *The Girl in Pink Tights* opens on Broadway.

Billy Graham begins his London Crusade on 1 March.

March 1954

Top: the USA's 15 megatonne Castle Bravo nuclear bomb is prepared for detonation. On 1 March (below) it is exploded off the Marshall Islands in the Pacific.

Saturday 6: US politician William Hays, who introduced the Hays Code for self-censorship of the film industry, dies aged 74.

Sunday 7: British olympic swimmer David Wilkie is born in Colombo, Ceylon.

Singer and presenter Cheryl Baker (Bucks Fizz) is born in London.

The second most senior member of Kenya's Mau Mau insurgency group surrenders to British colonial forces.

Monday 8: US forces acting in a support role with French troops in Laos come under attack as the Vietminh insurgency increases in ferocity.

Tuesday 9: The Hon Herb McKenley OM (Jamaica) sets the world record for the quarter mile sprint at 46.7 seconds at Bendigo, Australia.

Wednesday 10: Questions are raised in Parliament about the mounting expense of the new British Atomic Energy Authority.

Thursday 11: Doctors advise British Prime Minister Winston Churchill, 79, to retire following a health scare; he refuses and continues in office until April 1955.

Cheryl Baker of Bucks Fizz is born on 7 March.

March 1954

Friday 12: Arnold Schoenberg's opera *Moses and Aaron* is first performed, in Hamburg, West Germany.

Saturday 13: The Battle of Dien Bien Phu begins in Laos as the last major French colonial outpost comes under attack from Vietminh communist forces.

Sunday 14: At the 10th Inter-American Conference, the government of Brazil declares support for a US plan to prevent communism spreading in Latin America.

The popularity of smoking in the 1950s leads to health concerns: the American Cancer Society begins a study on 18 March.

Monday 15: US Vice President Richard Nixon tacitly attacks the McCarthy 'witch hunts', stating that any investigation into communist subversion in government must be 'fair' and 'proper'.

The Chords record their hit doo-wop song *Sh-boom*.

Tuesday 16: The singer and actor Jimmy Nail (*Auf Wiedersehn Pet, Evita*) is born in Newcastle Upon Tyne, County Durham.

Wednesday 17: French wartime leader Charles de Gaulle announces his disapproval of the proposed European army combining forces from six countries including France and West Germany.

The Chords record *Sh-boom* on 15 March.

March 1954

Thursday 18: The American Cancer Society begins a scientific study into a possible link between cigarette smoking and lung cancer.

I See the Moon by The Stargazers hits number one in the UK singles charts.

Friday 19: 18 USAF servicemen are killed when a Fairchild C119 'flying boxcar' transport plane crashes in bad weather near Annapolis, Maryland.

Saturday 20: The first boxing match to be broadcast on colour television takes place as middleweight Joey Giardello knocks out Willie Troy at the Madison Square Garden, New York City.

Sunday 21: US evangelist Billy Graham holds a special service at London's Harringay Arena, with screen cowboy Roy Rogers in attendance; it draws a crowd of 40,000.

Monday 22: The London Bullion Market reopens after being closed since 1939.

Tuesday 23: Vietminh forces cut off the remaining French colonial troops in Laos from supply lines as they capture the airstrip at Dien Bien Phu.

Gregory Peck and Audrey Hepburn in *Roman Holiday*, for which Hepburn wins an Oscar on 25 March

March 1954

The comedy film *Doctor in the House* starring Dirk Bogarde and Kenneth More is released.

Wednesday 24: Major French air attacks take place on massing Vietminh forces at Dien Bien Phu, the last colonial stronghold in Laos. An imminent ground attack is expected as hundreds of troops arrive from communist China.

Thursday 25: The 26th Academy Awards are held. *From Here to Eternity* wins Best Picture; William Holden wins Best Actor for *Stalag 17* and Audrey Hepburn wins Best Actress for *Roman Holiday*.

Dirk Bogarde stars in *Doctor in the House*, released on 23 April.

Friday 26: The US government pledges another 25 bomber planes for beleagured French troops in Laos.

Saturday 27: The first thermonuclear bomb test takes place on Bikini Atoll by US forces in the Pacific. The bomb is more destructive and smaller than early atomic weapons.

Sunday 28: The British troopship *Empire Windrush* catches fire off the coast of Algeria; all 1500 on board are evacuated.

Monday 29: Rear Admiral Robert A Theobald, US Navy (retired) claims that President Franklin Roosevelt deliberately forced Japan into the Second World War by refusing to act on warnings of the attack on Pearl Harbor.

Tuesday 30: Canada's first underground railway opens in Toronto.

Cricketer Sir Gary Sobers (West Indies) makes his test match debut aged just 17.

Wednesday 31: West Germany ratifies the European Defence Community Treaty.

April 1954

Thursday 1: The world's largest school, South Point, opens in Calcutta, India.

Cardiff Airport opens.

Friday 2: Plans are announced for a new theme park in California, to be named 'Disneyland'.

The BBC broadcasts the first British TV soap opera, *The Grove Family.*

Saturday 3: Oxford wins the 100th Boat Race.

The Soviet diplomat Vladimir Petrov defects and claims asylum in Australia.

Arturo Toscanini.

Sunday 4: Composer Arturo Toscanini, 87, gives his last concert performance, in Carnegie Hall, New York. The event is broadcast live on radio and, following a minor lapse by Toscanini, technicians panic and take the show off the air for one minute, making the mistake seem worse than it is.

April 1954

Rock and roll is born on 12 April as Bill Haley and His Comets record *Rock Around The Clock*.

Monday 5: Skirmishes between North and South Korean troops take place in the demilitarised border zone, which has been peaceful since the end of the Korean War in July 1953. China calls it a 'serious violation of the armistice'.

Tuesday 6: Britain's Prime Minister Winston Churchill reveals that a secret pact, now cancelled, was made with the USA in 1943 that the atom bomb would only be used with the consent of both the UK and USA.

Wednesday 7: US President Dwight D Eisenhower announces the 'domino theory', the idea that communism will spread through SE Asia as each country falls to it like dominoes in a row.

Thursday 8: 37 people are killed when three planes collide over Saskatchewan, Canada.

Friday 9: The Japanese film *Gate of Hell* wins the Grand Prix at the Cannes Film Festival.

Actor Dennis Quaid (*The Right Stuff*) is born in Houston, Texas.

Atom bomb creator J Robert Oppenheimer is investigated for Soviet links on 13 April.

April 1954

Saturday 10: Royal Tan ridden by Brian Marshall wins the Grand National.

Wales, England and France are joint winners of Rugby's Five Nations tournament.

Auguste Lumiere, creator of the first motion picture, dies aged 91.

Sunday 11: Achille Van Acker becomes Prime Minister of Belgium.

Raymond Impanis wins the Paris-Roubaix cycle race.

Aneurin Bevan resigns on 14 April.

Monday 12: Bill Haley and His Comets record *Rock Around the Clock*, widely regarded as the first 'rock and roll' song.

Tuesday 13: J Robert Oppenheimer, one of the scientists who developed the atom bomb, is investigated by the US government for possible Soviet collaboration. Charges are not proven but his security clearance is revoked.

Wednesday 14: Labour shadow minister Aneurin Bevan resigns over his party's support for the rearming of West Germany.

Doris Day hits number one in the charts on 22 April.

Thursday 15: 14 die when the Canadian ship *Chelan* sinks off the coast of Alaska.

Friday 16: (Good Friday) Actress Ellen Barkin (*Sea of Love*) is born in New York City.

Communist forces are reported to have advanced to within 3000 feet of the last French colonial stronghold at Dien Bien Phu, Laos.

Saturday 17: US Vice President Nixon announces that if French forces evacuate from Indochina, American troops may have to

April 1954

Soviet agents attempt to extradite Evdokia Petrova in Sydney on 19 April.

replace them in order to prevent the spread of communism in south east Asia.

Sunday 18: (Easter Sunday): Desperate French forces at Dien Bien Phu in Laos mount bayonet charges to repel encircling communist troops, despite being outnumbered three to one.

The ailing Pope Pius XII gives an Easter broadcast urging world leaders to turn the use of atomic energy from war to peace.

Monday 19: Two KGB officers attempt to extradite Evdokia Petrova, wife of the recently defected Soviet diplomat Vladimir Petrov, from Australia; the attempt is thwarted by large crowds of anti-communist demonstrators.

Tuesday 20: The last hanging takes place in the Republic of Ireland as Michael Manning, 25, is executed for murder.

Wednesday 21: Georgi Malenkov becomes premier of the USSR.

Thursday 22: As its colonial forces in Laos face defeat, the French government asks for international military assistance.

Secret Love by Doris Day hits number one in the UK singles charts.

Friday 23: 25 people are killed when an Argentine Airlines Douglas C-47 aeroplane crashes in Sierra de Vilgo, Argentina.

The documentary film maker Michael Moore is born in Flint, Michigan.

Georgi Malenkov becomes Soviet premier on 21 April.

April 1954

Saturday 24: Wolverhampton Wanderers becomes top of English football's First Division for the first time in the club's history.

Sunday 25: The first practical solar battery is launched by Bell Laboratories.

Monday 26: The cult Japanese film *The Seven Samurai* is released.

Tuesday 27: Celtic defeat Aberdeen 2-1 to win the 1953-4 Scottish Cup football competition.

Wednesday 28: Attempts to broker a ceasefire in the Indochina conflict begin at the Geneva Conference.

HM Queen Elizabeth II arrives in Uganda as part of her African tour; several thousand well-wishers turn out to greet her and Prince Philip despite objections from nationalist groups.

Thursday 29: The comedian Jerry Seinfeld is born in New York City.

Moscow breaks off diplomatic relations with Australia following the blocked extradition attempt of asylum seeker Evdokia Petrova on 19 April.

Friday 30: Darius Milhaud's 4th Concerto for Piano and Orchestra is first performed, in Haifa, Israel.

Poster for *The Seven Samurai*, released on 26 April.

May 1954

Charles Lindbergh, shown here after making the first solo transatlantic flight in 1927, wins the Pulitzer Prize on 3 May for his autobiography.

Saturday 1: West Bromwich Albion beats Preston North End 3-2 to win football's FA Cup Final at Wembley Stadium.

The American Motors Corporation (AMC) is formed by the merger of Nash-Kelvinator and Hudson Motors.

The Unification Church, better known as the Moonies, is formed in South Korea under Reverend Sun Myung Moon.

Sunday 2: Communist forces in Laos breach part of the defences of the French base at Dien Bien Phu; the French high command describe the situation as 'very serious'.

Monday 3: The BBC's *Blue Peter* presenter Peter Duncan is born in London.

The aviator Charles Lindbergh is awarded the Pulitzer Prize for Biography for his book *The Spirit of St Louis*.

Tuesday 4: Further attacks by Vietminh forces on the French

May 1954

base at Dien Bien Phu in Laos leave French troops divided into two sections with no way of reaching each other.

Wednesday 5: President Federico Chavez of Paraguay is ousted in a military coup.

Thursday 6: Dr Roger Bannister becomes the first man to run a mile in under four minutes, at Iffley, Oxford. Bannister achieves the feat despite having spent the morning working in his medical practice in London.

Such a Night by Johnny Ray hits number one in the UK singles charts.

Friday 7: The 11,721 occupants of the French garrison at Dien Bien Phu, Laos, surrender after holding out for nearly two months against Vietminh forces. A final radio transmission states 'The enemy have over-run us...*Vive La France*!'

Roger Bannister runs the four minute mile on 6 May.

Saturday 8: The 1954 County Cricket Championship opens in England and Wales.

French troops are marched to a POW camp in Laos after the surrender at Dien Bien Phu on 7 May.

May 1954

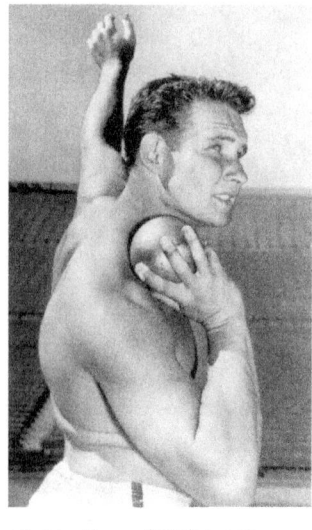

Above: Parry O'Brien sets the world shot-put record on 8 May.

Below: Johnny Ray hits number one in the charts on 6 May.

Parry O'Brien (USA) becomes the first shot-putter to throw to over 60' (18.29m) in Los Angeles, California.

Sunday 9: The French government's request for a UN-enforced ceasefire in Indochina following the fall of Dien Bien Phu on 7 May is blocked by Soviet delegates at the Geneva peace conference.

Police in Fredericksburg, Virginia, are reported to have foiled an assassination attempt on President Dwight Eisenhower during his visit to the town.

Monday 10: The Bolshoi Ballet's first visit to France since the Second World War is cancelled due to ill-feeling towards the Soviet Union after the defeat of French forces in Laos by communists on 7 May.

Tuesday 11: US Secretary of State John Foster Dulles strongly indicates that there will be no US military intervention to support France's rule in Indochina.

Wednesday 12: Actor Gary Cooper is badly injured on set by a misfiring gun whilst filming *Veracruz*.

Thursday 13: Eurovision singer Johnny Logan is born in Melbourne, Australia.

Mikhail Botvinnik (USSR) wins the World Chess Championship in Moscow.

May 1954

The first Boeing 707 is brought out at Renton, Washington, on 14 May.

Friday 14: The prototype of the Boeing 707 jet airliner is first flown.

Saturday 15: The Latin Union is formed in Madrid to promote the use of the five Romance languages worldwide (French, Spanish, Italian, Romanian and Portuguese).

Sunday 16: A large scale uprising takes place in a Soviet labour camp (gulag) in Kengir, Khazakstan; the rebellion lasts for a month before finally being put down by the army.

Monday 17: The US Supreme Court rules that racial segregation in public (state) schools is unconstitutional.

Tuesday 18: 56 die when the communist gunboat *Rujin* is sunk by Chinese nationalist forces.

Wednesday 19: Pakistan and the USA sign a mutual defence agreement.

Thursday 20: Chinese nationalist leader Chang Kai Shek is re-elected.

Friday 21: The 1954 Giro D'Italia bicycle race begins.

Saturday 22: Johnny Adams wins the 79th Preakness Stakes horse race on Hasty Road.

Chang Kai Shek is re-elected on 20 May.

May 1954

Ferenc Puskás leads the Hungarian defeat of England on 23 May.

Robert Capa is killed in Indochina on 25 May.

Sunday 23: In a friendly match held in Budapest, England is beaten 7-1 by Hungary under the command of Ferenc Puskás. It remains England's worst football defeat.

Monday 24: A Viking 11 rocket launched from White Sands, New Mexico, reaches a record altitude of 158 miles (254km).

Tuesday 25: The photojournalist Robert Capa is killed, age 40, by a land mine while reporting on the Indochina war.

Wednesday 26: In one of the worst peacetime military disasters in US history, 103 die in a fire on board the USS *Bennington* off the coast of Massachusetts.

Thursday 27: The comedian Charlie Chaplin and composer Dimitri Shostakovich are jointly awarded the World Peace Prize by the communist-sponsored World Peace Council.

Friday 28: The US military sends 17 more fighter planes to bolster French forces in Indochina as communist troops advance on the colonial capital of Hanoi.

Saturday 29: The Liberal Party under Prime Minister Robert

May 1954

Menzies is re-elected for a fourth term in Australia's federal election.

The first meeting of the secretive Bilderberg Group of financiers takes place in Oosterbeek in the Netherlands.

Diane Leather (GB) becomes the first woman to run a mile in under five minutes.

Tony Trabert and Maureen Connolly win the French Open tennis tournament.

Sunday 30: 23 die when the passenger ferry *Pajtas* sinks on Lake Balaton, Hungary.

Monday 31: Bill Vukovich wins the Indianapolis 500 motor race.

Robert Menzies is re-elected on 29 May.

June 1954

Tuesday 1: The Republican senator for Vermont, Ralph Flanders, attacks Senator Joseph McCarthy for his 'Hitler-like' methods in hunting for communists in the US government.

Wednesday 2: John A Costello becomes Taoiseach (Prime Minister) of the Republic of Ireland.

Thursday 3: 50 French bombing planes destroy a Vietminh base set up for the invasion of nearby Hanoi, the colonial capital of Vietnam.

Friday 4: USAF pilot Major Arthur 'Kit' Murray sets a new altitude record of 89,810 feet (17 miles) in a Bell X-1A rocket plane.

Major Arthur Murray sets an air record on 4 June.

Saturday 5: Pope Pius XII publishes the encyclical *Ecclesiae Fastos*.

Sunday 6: The Eurovision TV network goes into operation in the UK and Europe; it later launches the Eurovision Song Contest.

June 1954

Monday 7: The mathematician and computing pioneer Alan Turing commits suicide, aged 41.

Tuesday 8: In the Geneva peace talks, Soviet foreign minister Molotov accuses the USA of deliberately prolonging the war in Indochina.

Wednesday 9: US Army lawyer Joseph Welch lashes out at Senator Joseph McCarthy during an enquiry into communism in the armed forces, saying 'have you no sense of decency?'

Juan Manuel Fangio wins the Belgian Grand Prix on 20 June.

Thursday 10: Extensive French counter-offensives take place around Hanoi, Vietnam, as Vietminh forces prepare a full onslaught on the capital.

Friday 11: US President Eisenhower announces in a speech that world communism may last another 40 years. His prediction is almost correct, as the USSR is dissolved in 1991.

Saturday 12: A major arms raid by the IRA takes place at Gough Barracks in Armagh; 340 rifles and 62 machine guns are stolen in broad daylight.

Sunday 13: Carlo Cerci wins the 1954 Giro d'Italia bicycle race.

Monday 14: The words 'under God' are added to the US Pledge of Allegiance.

Tuesday 15: The Union of European Football Associations (UEFA), is formed in Basel, Switzerland.

Left: Senator McCarthy comes under attack on 9 June.

June 1954

Wednesday 16: The 1954 FIFA World Cup football competition opens in Lausanne, Switzerland.

Thursday 17: The suitably named Pierre Mendès France is elected Prime Minister of France.

A military coup led by Carlos Castillo Armas takes place in Guatemala.

Friday 18: The 4th Berlin International Film Festival opens.

Saturday 19: Ed Furgol wins the US Open golf championship.

The actress Kathleen Turner (*Romancing the Stone*) is born in Springfield, Missouri.

Sunday 20: Juan Manuel Fangio wins the Belgian Grand Prix motor race.

Monday 21: Engineer Gideon Sundback, who perfected the design of Whitcomb Judson's prototype Slide Fastener (better known as the zipper or zip) dies aged 74.

The American Cancer Society releases a report showing for the first time that heavy cigarette smoking is linked to lung cancer.

Tuesday 22: The comedian Jackie Gleason and his wife Genevieve are awarded a legal separation.

The architect Buckminster Fuller (second from left) demonstrates his model of a geodesic dome to students. He patents the design on 29 June.

June 1954

French soldiers surrender at the Battle of Mang Yang Pass on 24 June.

Wednesday 23: The new French prime minister Pierre France announces he is 'optimistic' about peace in French Indochina following a meeting with Chinese communist officials in Geneva.

Thursday 24: The Battle of Mang Yang Pass begins in Vietnam between colonial French forces and Vietminh communist rebels.

Friday 25: 50 people are killed when Hurricane Alice hits Texas.

Saturday 26: The world's first nuclear power station opens, in Obninsk, USSR.

Sunday 27: Hungary beats Brazil 4-2 in a violent World Cup quarter-final match.

Monday 28: The newspaper columnist AA Gill is born in Edinburgh (died 2016).

Tuesday 29: Architect Buckminster Fuller patents the geodesic dome.

Wednesday 30: A solar eclipse is visible across the northern USA, Canada and northern Europe.

July 1954

Thursday 1: The Japan Self Defence Forces are set up, allowing a limited army, navy and air force following the country's demilitarisation after 1945.

Friday 2: A poll of Welsh local authorities indicates Cardiff as the favoured location of the new Welsh capital. It becomes the capital in 1955.

Saturday 3: The American artist Reginald Marsh dies aged 56.

Babe Didrikson-Zaharias wins the US Open women's golf championships.

Left: a butcher in Oswestry, Shropshire, celebrates the end of meat rationing with his customers on 4 July.

July 1954

Maureen Connolly wins Wimbledon on 3 July.

Maureen Connolly (USA) defeats fellow American Louise Brough to win the Wimbledon ladies' tennis final.

Sunday 4: Meat rationing in Britain is lifted, ending the last restrictions on food purchasing in place since the Second World War.

Monday 5: The BBC broadcasts its first television news bulletin.

Elvis Presley's first single, *That's All Right*, is recorded by Sun Records in Memphis, Tennessee.

Tuesday 6: A 15 year old boy, Raymond Kuchenmeister, is shot dead by an airline pilot after he attempts to hijack at gunpoint an American Airlines plane in New York City. His .38 calibre pistol is later found to be unloaded.

Wednesday 7: WHBQ in Memphis, Tennessee, becomes the first radio station in the world to broadcast a record by Elvis Presley.

Thursday 8: Boxer George Gardiner, the world's first Light Heavyweight champion, dies aged 77.

Cara Mia by David Whitfield with Mantovani and His Orchestra hits number one in the UK singles charts.

David Whitfield tops the charts on 8 July.

Friday 9: Design work begins on the X-15, the first hypersonic near-space rocket plane.

July 1954

Saturday 10: Peter Thomson becomes the first Australian to win the British Open men's golf championships at Royal Birkdale.

All Americans are warned to leave Vietnam as communist forces close in on the French colonial capital, Hanoi.

Sunday 11: 15 die and thousands are made homeless as the River Danube floods in Hungary, Austria and Czechoslovakia.

Frida Kahlo dies on 13 July.

Monday 12: Britain's Prime Minister Winston Churchill announces he is backing the US decision not to admit communist China into the United Nations.

Tuesday 13: The Mexican artist Frida Kahlo dies aged 47.

Wednesday 14: An RAF Victor bomber plane crashes near Cranfield, Bedfordshire, with the loss of all crew.

Thursday 15: The Argentinian racing driver Juan Fangio sets the lap record at Silverstone at an average of 100.35 mph (161.5 kph).

The saucy seaside postcard artist Donald McGill is prosecuted for obscenity; the ruling leads to many cards being destroyed.

Friday 16: A partial lunar eclipse takes place, visible from most of the western hemisphere.

Left: a Donald McGill postcard. The artist is prosecuted for obscenity on 15 July.

July 1954

Saturday 17: Angela Merkel, Chancellor of Germany, is born in Hamburg.

The notorious gangster George 'Machine Gun' Kelly dies aged 59.

Sunday 18: France's Prime Minister Pierre Mendes France announces that if he is unable to broker a ceasefire in Indochina by Tuesday, he will resign, and warns that an escalation of hostilities in the region may require the introduction of conscription.

Monday 19: Elvis Presley's first single, *That's All Right* is released in the USA.

The UK Atomic Energy Authority is set up, with the aim of building Britain's first nuclear power station.

Tuesday 20: A ceasefire in Indochina is brokered at the Geneva Conference. Vietnam is partitioned into communist north and capitalist south, with all French forces scheduled to withdraw.

Wednesday 21: The US military begins the immediate withdrawal of all its forces from Indochina.

A ceasefire is brokered in Indochina at the Geneva Conference on 20 July.

July 1954

Miriam Stevenson becomes Miss Universe on 24 July.

Thursday 22: In the Geneva peace conference, the United States refuses to endorse the Franco-Chinese peace settlement for Indochina.

Friday 23: The French Indochina government announces plans to evacuate 300,000 people from communist North Vietnam to the south.

Saturday 24: Miriam Stevenson (USA) is crowned Miss Universe in Long Beach, California.

10 die when a Cathay Pacific Douglas DC4 airliner is shot down by Chinese fighter planes in an unprovoked attack off Hainan Island.

Sunday 25: Chinese communist officials admit responsibility for the shooting down of the Cathay Pacific airliner the previous day, claiming it was a mistake.

Monday 26: East German authorities arrest 300 people in a clampdown on alleged American spies in the country.

Lt Genevieve de Galard, French army nurse hailed as the 'Angel of Dien Bien Phu' for her bravery under communist attack in Indochina, becomes the first woman to be an 'Honoured Guest' of the US Congress.

Lt de Galard becomes the first female 'Honoured Guest' on 26 July.

Tuesday 27: Britain agrees with Egypt to withdraw its 80,000

July 1954

troops from the Suez Canal zone, bringing to a close 72 years of British rule in the region.

Wednesday 28: The award-winning film *On the Waterfront* starring Marlon Brando is released.

Thursday 29: The first volume of JRR Tolkein's *Lord of the Rings* series, *Fellowship of the Ring*, is published.

Friday 30: The Fifth British Empire and Commonwealth Games opens in Vancouver, Canada.

The Television Act 1954 receives Royal Assent; this leads to Britain's first commercial television channel (ITV) in 1955.

Saturday 31: Lino Lacedelli and Achille Compagnoni of Italy become the first climbers to reach the summit of K2, the world's second highest mountain.

Lacedelli and Compagnoni, shown here suffering from frostbite, conquer K2 on 31 July.

August 1954

Sunday 1: France offers independence to Tunisia, on condition that all armed resistance to French rule is ended.

Monday 2: Joseph Cort, a US citizen working as a lecturer at the University of Birmingham, England, defects to the eastern bloc by claiming asylum on a Polish ship in London.

Tuesday 3: The French novelist Sidonie Gabrielle Colette (known simply as 'Colette') dies aged 81.

Britain's nuclear deterrent goes into operation with the launch of 1321 Flight RAF, using Vickers Valiant aeroplanes armed with 'Blue Danube' atom bombs.

Wednesday 4: Britain's Independent Television Authority goes into operation.

The English Electric P1 supersonic fighter plane is first flown.

Left: the RAF' English Electric P1 fighter plane is first flown on 4 August by test pilot Roland Beaumont (inset).

August 1954

Thursday 5: The Shah of Iran agrees to end a three year dispute with Britain over the rights to sell Iran's oil.

Salad Days, one of the most popular West End musicals of the decade, opens in London.

Friday 6: The German airline Lufthansa is formed; it goes into operation in 1955.

Saturday 7: Christian Dior launches its 'flat look' brassiere, toning down the highly prominent female silhouette of the late 1940s/early 1950s.

Sunday 8: British newspapers are filled with speculation after Princess Margaret is invited to stay with aristocrat Colin Tennant; rumours are unfounded as the Princess eventually marries Anthony Armstrong-Jones in 1960.

Cigarette card showing Sir Gordon Richards, who retires on 10 August.

Monday 9: 30 people are killed when a Lockheed Constellation airliner crashes in the Azores; it is Portugal's second worst aviation disaster to this date.

Tuesday 10: The British jockey Sir Gordon Richards retires following a record 4870 winning rides.

The First Indochina War officially ends at 08.00.

Wednesday 11: India forceably annexes the Portuguese colonies of Dadra and Nagar Haveli; the small enclaves are guarded only by a handful of police constables.

Thursday 12: Francois Hollande, 24th President of France, is born in Rouen.

French author Colette dies on 3 August.

August 1954

Above: *Sports Illustrated* is first published on 16 August.

Above: Former British PM Clement Atlee heads a delegation to China on 16 August.

Friday 13: The US government grants asylum to top Soviet defector Yuri Rastvorov.

Saturday 14: Portuguese forces rush to defend their colony of Goa against possible takeover by India, following the seizure of the Dadra and Nagar Haveli colonies on 11 August.

Sunday 15: The General Assembly of the World Council of Churches meets in Evanston, Illinois.

Monday 16: The first issue of *Sports Illustrated* is published in the USA.

A British Labour Party delegation led by former Prime Minister Clement Atlee visits the Chinese Communist Party in Peking.

Tuesday 17: British Prime Minister Winston Churchill convenes an emergency meeting to save the proposed European Army, as the European Defence Community fails to agree on a workable plan for its inception.

Wednesday 18: An exchange of POWs in Indochina is proposed by Vietminh communist guerillas, including the release of the commander of French colonial forces, Brigadier General Christian de Castries.

August 1954

The Lockheed C130 heavy transporter plane makes its first flight on 23 August.

Thursday 19: The Communist Party of the USA is outlawed.

Friday 20: 52 people are injured in an anti-British demonstration in Athens, Greece, as protestors demand the return of Cyprus to Greek rule.

Saturday 21: Plans for a European army are called off as France and West Germany fail to agree.

Sunday 22: 12 people are killed when a Braniff Airways Douglas C47 airliner crashes near Mason City, Iowa.

Monday 23: The Lockheed C130 Hercules makes its first flight.

Tuesday 24: Gartulio Vargas, President of Brazil, commits suicide following accusations of conspiring to murder a political opponent.

Wednesday 25: The 1954 European Athletics Championships opens in Berne, Switzerland.

Captain Joseph C McConnell USAF, the top scoring jet fighter ace, is killed when his F-86H Sabre malfunctions

Christian de Castries, captured head of French forces in Indochina; the Vietminh offer to release him on 18 August.

August 1954

over Edwards Air Force Base, California.

Thursday 26: The BBC radio presenter Steve Wright is born in Greenwich, London.

Friday 27: The US military announces all its fighter jets will be withdrawn from South Korea following the end of the Korean War.

Saturday 28: It is announced that HMCS *Labrador* has become the first warship to traverse the Northwest Passage in the Arctic.

Sunday 29: San Francisco International Airport opens.

US air ace Capt Joseph McConnell is killed on 25 August when his plane malfunctions.

Monday 30: 68 die when Hurricane Carol hits the US east coast.

Tuesday 31: The Canadian government closes its UFO monitoring station near Ottawa, stating that it is too expensive to run and has sighted nothing since being set up in 1953.

September 1954

Wednesday 1: The World Council of Churches conference closes after 17 days with a plea for Christian unity.

Kidbrooke School in Greenwich, London, opens as Britain's first comprehensive (all-ability) school.

Thursday 2: The Alfred Hitchcock directed thriller *Rear Window*, starring James Stewart and Grace Kelly, is released.

Friday 3: The last episode of the *Lone Ranger* radio series is broadcast in the USA.

The National Trust for Scotland purchases Fair Isle.

Saturday 4: Champion strongman Peter Cortes performs a one-arm deadlift of 370lbs, (167kg) over triple his bodyweight, in York, Pennsylvania. Even more remarkable is that Cortes has only one lung.

Sunday 5: 28 die when KLM Flight 633 crashes near Shannon, Ireland.

Grace Kelly and James Stewart star in *Rear Window*, released on 2 September.

September 1954

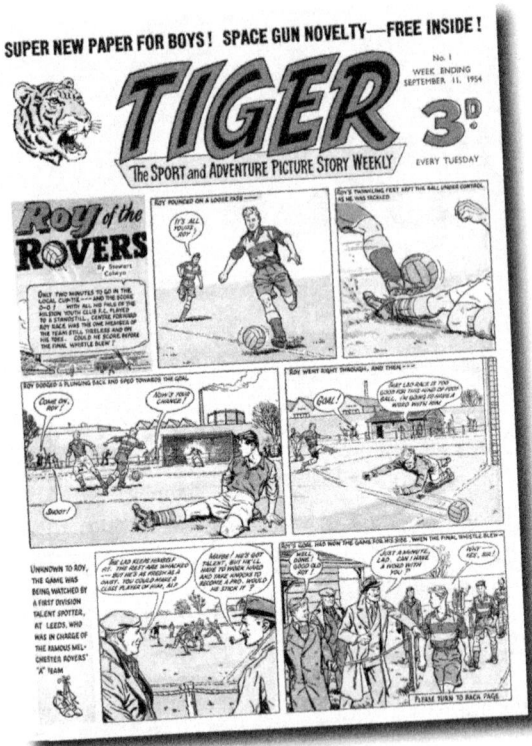

Roy of the Rovers makes his first appearance in *Tiger* comic on 11 September.

Monday 6: Britain's Prime Minister Winston Churchill cuts short his summer holiday to try to arrange new talks on the formation of a European army.

Tuesday 7: Cartoonist Bud Fisher, creator of the newspaper strip Mutt and Jeff, dies aged 69.

Major sea and air battles rage between Chinese nationalist and communist forces at Quenoy, Taiwan.

Wednesday 8: The Southeast Asia Treaty Organisation (SEATO) mutual defence pact is signed in Manila, Phillipines.

Thursday 9: 1500 die in an earthquake in Orleansville, Algeria.

Friday 10: The USA, Britain and France reject Soviet proposals for a combined European defence treaty.

Saturday 11: The Miss America beauty pageant is broadcast on television for the first time.

The long running cartoon strip *Roy of the Rovers* is first published, in the *Tiger* comic.

September 1954

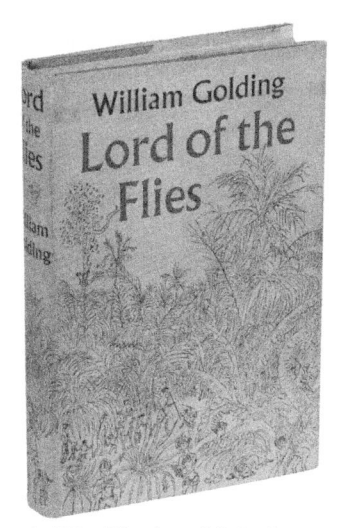

Lord of the Flies is published on 17 September.

Sunday 12: US Secretary of State Alan Dulles announces that any attempt by communist China to seize the nationalist stronghold of Formosa (Taiwan) will be met by US resistance.

Monday 13: Potholers Jean Cadoux and Georges Garby descend a record 2485 feet (757 metres) at the Berger caves near Grenoble, France.

Tuesday 14: Benjamin Britten's opera *Turn of the Screw* premieres in Venice.

Wednesday 15: Britain's foreign secretary Anthony Eden visits Italy to win support for a European defence pact.

The British government sets up the Wolfenden Committee to investigate the liberalisation of homosexual and prostitution offences.

Thursday 16: Lewis Strauss, chairman of the United States Atomic Energy Commission, announces that in the future nuclear energy will be 'too cheap to meter.'

Little Things Mean A Lot by Kitty Kallen hits number one in the UK singles charts.

Friday 17: William Golding's novel *Lord of the Flies* is published.

Kitty Kallen tops the charts on 16 September.

September 1954

Left: on 22 September, West German Leader Konrad Adenaur calls for the abolition of Allied occupation sectors such as those shown far left in West Berlin.

Saturday 18: The Last Night of the Proms in London for the first time features the now traditional programme of *Land of Hope and Glory, Jerusalem* and *Rule, Britannia.*

The Roman temple of Mithras is discovered buried beneath Walbrook, London EC4.

Sunday 19: A nine-power European defence conference, organised by Britain and the USA, is announced.

Monday 20: 'Prayers and parachutes' are credited with saving 15 military chaplains and 3 crewmen who manage to jump to safety from their burning C46 transport plane just before it crashes near Los Angeles, California.

Tuesday 21: Shinzo Abe, Prime Minister of Japan, is born in Tokyo (died 2022).

Wednesday 22: West German Chancellor Konrad Adenaur demands the end of Allied military occupation, in place since 1945, and full sovereignty for his country.

Terence Rattigan's play *Separate Tables* premieres in London.

Thursday 23: Edward Pilgrim, 49, of Romford, Essex, becomes a *cause célèbre* after committing suicide in protest against the compulsory purchase of his land to build council flats.

September 1954

Friday 24: Following a fact finding visit to communist China, Britain's Labour Party leader Clement Atlee urges the west to 'get rid' of nationalist leader Chiang Kai Shek immediately.

Saturday 25: The actress Audrey Hepburn marries actor Mel Ferrer in Switzerland.

Sunday 26: 1505 die when the ferry *Toya Maru* sinks after being caught in Typhoon Marie off the coast of Japan.

Monday 27: The world's first late night TV talk show, *The Tonight Show*, is broadcast on NBC in the USA.

Audrey Hepburn marries Mel Ferrer on 25 September.

Tuesday 28: The comedy film *The Belles of St Trinians*, starring Alistair Sim, is released.

A dock strike begins in London; over the following month it escalates into a paralysing national dispute.

Wednesday 29: The European Organisation for Nuclear Research (CERN) is formed.

Thursday 30: The world's first nuclear submarine, the USS *Nautilus*, is commissioned following its launch in January.

Joyce Grenfell stars in *The Belles of St Trinians*, released on 28 September.

October 1954

Friday 1: The British colony of Nigeria becomes the Federation of Nigeria, with limited self rule, under Governor General Sir John Stuart Macpherson.

Saturday 2: The 1954 World Series baseball championship is won by the New York Giants.

Sunday 3: The long running sitcom *Father Knows Best* is first shown on US TV.

The western Allies agree to end the occupation of West Germany and to allow it limited re-armament.

The sitcom *Father Knows Best* is first shown on 3 October. It stars (clockwise from left) Billy Gray, Jane Wyatt, Robert Young, Elinor Donahue and Lauren Chapin.

October 1954

The Trieste-Italy border. It is abolished on 5 October as the Free City of Trieste comes under Italian rule.

Monday 4: Hollywood star Marilyn Monroe announces she is getting a divorce from baseball legend Joe DiMaggio after just nine months of marriage.

Tuesday 5: The Free City of Trieste, a disputed territory between Italy and Yugoslavia, goes under Italian rule.

Wednesday 6: In a last-ditch attempt to prevent the re-arming of West Germany, the USSR government offers to withdraw all its troops from East Germany; the offer is not accepted.

Thursday 7: 37 die when the freighter *Mormackite* sinks off the coast of Virginia, USA.

Friday 8: Soviet foreign minister Vyacheslav Molotov tells a crowd of 50,000 in East Berlin that they must choose between German re-armament, or German reunification. Reunification does not take place until 1990.

Molotov gives the East Germans a stark choice on 8 October.

October 1954

Robert Preston and Kim Hunter star in the Broadway play *The Tender Trap* which opens on 13 October.

Vietminh communist troops enter Hanoi, Vietnam, just hours after the withdrawal of French colonial forces according to the Geneva peace plan.

Saturday 9: The last survivors of the *Mormackite*, which sank on 7 October, are picked up from life rafts after surviving attacks by man-eating sharks.

Sunday 10: Carlos Castillo Armas becomes President of Guatemala.

Monday 11: French colonial rule in Vietnam formally ends; the administration of the north goes to the Vietminh communists, and the south to the government of Ngo Din Diem.

Left: Ngo Din Diem (second from left) with his senior ministers take over South Vietnam on 11 October.

October 1954

Emperor Haile Selassie visits Britain on 14 October.

An estimated 1000 people are killed when Hurricane Hazel crosses the island of Haiti.

Tuesday 12: Daniel Malan resigns as Prime Minister of South Africa.

Wednesday 13: The romantic comedy play *The Tender Trap* opens on Broadway.

Chris Chataway (GB) sets the world record for running 5000m at 13 minutes 51.6 seconds at White City, London.

Thursday 14: The first American four-stage rocket is launched, from Wallops Island, Virginia.

Hold My Hand by Don Cornell hits number one in the UK singles charts.

The Emperor Haile Selassie of Ethiopia makes a state visit to Britain.

Don Cornell tops the charts on 14 October.

Friday 15: Hurricane Hazel hits the continental USA; it is on record as the most northerly category 4 hurricane, reaching as far as North Carolina.

Saturday 16: Elvis Presley makes his first radio broadcast, on the *Louisiana Hayride* show on station KWKH from Shreveport, Lousiana.

Sunday 17: The first major civil defence evacuation exercise in the USA takes place in Erie, Pennsylvania (pop.130,000); however, poor weather and general apathy leads to only 15% of

October 1954

The first pocket transistor radio (shown here with leather case) is launched on 18 October.

the population leaving their homes after a simulated nuclear attack warning.

Monday 18: The Regency TR-1, the world's first transistor radio, is announced.

The newspaper cartoon strip *Hi and Lois* is first published in the USA.

Tuesday 19: The region of Exmoor in south-west England becomes a national park.

British rule in Egypt formally ends.

Wednesday 20: The musical *Peter Pan* starring Mary Martin and Cyril Ritchard opens on Broadway.

Thursday 21: A break to the paralysing dock strike in Britain is in sight as union leaders and dock owners agree to talks.

Friday 22: Cartoonist George McManus, creator of the newspaper strip *Bringing Up Father,* dies aged 70. The strip, started by McManus in 1913, is continued by other artists after his death until 2000.

Saturday 23: West Germany joins NATO.

Ernest Hemingway wins the Nobel Prize for Literature on 28 October.

October 1954

Sunday 24: Mike Hawthorn (GB) wins the Spanish Grand Prix, the last such race to be held in Spain until 1967.

Monday 25: 300 people are killed in landslides following heavy rain in Salerno, Italy.

Tuesday 26: *Disneyland*, the first Disney TV show, is broadcast on ABC in the USA.

A failed assassination attempt takes place on Egyptian leader General Gamal Abdel Nasser by a member of the Muslim Brotherhood.

French troops patrol in an Algerian village following the outbreak of war on 31 October.

Wednesday 27: An angry mob in Cairo, Egypt, burns down the headquarters of the Muslim Brotherhood after one of its members attempted to assassinate the country's leader on 26 October.

Thursday 28: The Nobel Prize for Literature is awarded to Ernest Hemingway for *The Old Man and the Sea*.

Friday 29: The thriller writer Lee Child (creator of Jack Reacher) is born in Coventry.

HM Queen Elizabeth the Queen Mother visits New York City.

Saturday 30: 42 are missing, presumed dead, when a US Navy Lockheed Constellation aeroplane crashes off the coast of Maryland.

Sunday 31: The Algerian War of Independence begins.

November 1954

Monday 1: General Batista of Cuba is re-elected as President after a probably rigged vote.

Pondicherry and the other colonies of French India come under Indian control.

Tuesday 2: The radio comedy *Hancock's Half Hour*, starring Tony Hancock, is first broadcast by the BBC.

Wednesday 3: The first *Godzilla* film premieres in Tokyo, Japan.

The painter Henri Matisse dies aged 84.

Tony Hancock's radio comedy starts on 2 November.

Thursday 4: The world's fastest seaplane, the Convair Seadart, explodes over San Diego Bay, California, during an air show. Pilot Charles E Richbourg is found alive in the sea but dies shortly afterwards.

Friday 5: The state of war between Japan and Burma, in place since 1942, is formally ended as Japan pays $250m in war reparations to the former British colony.

Saturday 6: Baron Konstantin Von Neurath, Hitler's foreign

November 1954

The Iwo Jima Memorial is dedicated on 10 November.

minister, is released from Spandau prison on grounds of ill health.

Sunday 7: Russian jet fighters shoot down a USAF B29 aircraft off the coast of Japan, claiming the Americans were spying; 1 crew member is killed but the remaining ten parachute to safety.

Monday 8: The Anglo-Japanese author Sir Kazuo Ishiguro (*Remains of the Day*) is born in Nagasaki, Japan.

Tuesday 9: A devastating typhoon with winds of over 120mph hits the Philippines.

Wednesday 10: US President Dwight D Eisenhower dedicates the Iwo Jima Memorial at Arlington National Cemetery.

Thursday 11: Armistice Day in the USA is changed to Veterans' Day.

Friday 12: New York City's Ellis Island immigration centres closes.

Saturday 13: Sidney Holland's National Party wins the New Zealand general election.

Great Britain beats France to win the first ever Rugby League World Cup, in Paris.

Fabian of the Yard, the first British TV police procedural series, is first broadcast.

A technician with an animated model used in the film *Godzilla*, released on 3 November.

November 1954

Sunday 14: 40 die when the Chinese nationalist warship *Tai Ping* is sunk by communist forces off the Tachen Islands.

Monday 15: The actor Lionel Barrymore dies aged 76.

Tuesday 16: The first regular transatlantic air route across the Arctic, rather than via the Azores, goes into service.

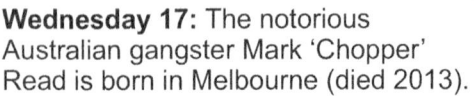

Lionel Barrymore (shown here as Mr Potter in *It's A Wonderful Life* dies on 15 November.

Wednesday 17: The notorious Australian gangster Mark 'Chopper' Read is born in Melbourne (died 2013).

French Prime Minister Pierre Mendes France meets US President Eisenhower for talks in Washington.

Thursday 18: 700 members of Hollywood's movie aristocracy attend the funeral of Lionel Barrymore at Calvary Cemetery, Los Angeles.

Friday 19: The government of West Germany agrees to join the western defence alliance and to begin the process of rearmament.

Saturday 20: Aircraft designer Clive Cessna, founder of the Cessna Corporation, dies aged 74.

Chinese nationalist forces make major bombing raids on communist troop bases on Toumen Island near Formosa (Taiwan).

Sunday 21: HMCS *Labrador* becomes the first warship to circumnavigate North America.

Bruce Seton stars as *Fabian of the Yard*, first broadcast on 13 November.

November 1954

Monday 22: The United States Supreme Court rules in Berman v Parker that private property can be compulsorily purchased by the federal government, in order to carry out a nationwide programme of slum clearance.

Tuesday 23: The Dow Jones Industrial Average reaches its highest point since 1929, just before the Wall Street Crash.

Wednesday 24: 20,000 French troops are sent to Algeria as the Arab uprising worsens.

Thursday 25: Malev, the Hungarian state airline, is formed.

Friday 26: 12 die when the Dutch ship *Tarpo* sinks off the coast of Cornwall, England.

Saturday 27: Seven die when the South Goodwin Lightship capsizes off the Kent coast.

Sunday 28: Physicist Enrico Fermi, creator of the first nuclear reactor, dies aged 53.

Monday 29: The music hall star George Robey, whose greatest hit was *If You Were the Only Girl in the World*, dies aged 85.

Tuesday 30: A meteorite weighing 9lb (4kg) crashes through the roof of a house in Sylacauga, Alabama, and hits Mrs Ann Hodges, 34, who is sleeping inside. It is the only recorded case of injury by an object from space.

French commandos in Algeria. On 24 November 20,000 extra troops are sent to the colony as the Arab uprising intensifies.

December 1954

Wednesday 1: The first Hyatt hotel, also the world's first to be built in an airport, opens in Los Angeles International Airport.

Thursday 2: The US senate votes 67-22 to condemn Senator Joseph McCarthy for his 'witch hunt' against suspected communists in government.

This Ole House by Rosemary Clooney hits number one in the UK singles charts.

Friday 3: William Walton's opera *Troilus and Cressida* opens in London.

Rosemary Clooney tops the charts on 2 December.

Saturday 4: The world's first Burger King restaurant opens in Miami, Florida.

Sunday 5: Anti-rearmament socialists win large gains in West Berlin's municipal elections.

Monday 6: The *Prix Goncourt,* the top French writing award, goes to Simone de Beauvoir for her novel The Mandarins.

Tuesday 7: After years of worsening air pollution, the city of Los

December 1954

Angeles appoints a 'smog controller' to tackle emissions.

Wednesday 8: 19 die when a Greek air force transporter plane crashes at Elefsis Air Base, Greece.

Thursday 9: Communist China condemns a new US defence pact with nationalist China (Taiwan), stating it will lead to 'grave consequences.'

Let's Have a Party by pianist Winifred Atwell hits number one in the UK singles charts.

US Navy women reserves with the 12' anchor of the USS *Forrestal*, launched on 11 December.

Friday 10: Colonel John Stapp, US Air Force, becomes the fastest human on earth to this date when he rides a rocket-powered test sledge at 632 mph (1017 kmh) at Holloman Air Force Base, New Mexico.

Saturday 11: Singer Jermaine Jackson of the Jackson Five is born in Gary, Indiana.

John Stapp becomes the fastest man on earth on 10 December on a rocket sled.

December 1954

The world's largest warship, the supercarrier USS *Forrestal* is launched.

Sunday 12: Pope Pius XII, suffering from an incapacitating mystery illness, is warned by doctors he must reduce his workload.

Monday 13: England wins the European Rugby League Championship.

Tuesday 14: A search begins for the MV *Southern Districts*, a freighter with 24 on board, which has not been heard of for several days. No trace is ever found other than a single lifejacket. It is eventually thought to have sunk in the infamous Bermuda Triangle.

Pope Pius XII suffers a mystery illness on 12 December.

Wednesday 15: The Dutch colony of Curacao becomes the Netherlands Antilles, with equal legal status to the Netherlands.

Thursday 16: Anti-British rioting breaks out in Athens as Britain refuses to allow its colony of Cyprus to come under Greek control.

Friday 17: UN Secretary Dag Hammarskjold announces talks with communist China to negotiate the release of 11 US airmen being held as spies.

Saturday 18: 26 people are killed when an Alitalia Douglas DC6B airliner crashes near Idlewild Airport (now John F Kennedy Airport), New York.

The actor Ray Liotta is born in Newark, New Jersey (died 2022)

Sunday 19: Five Royal Navy climbers die in an attempt to climb Ben Nevis, Britain's highest mountain.

December 1954

Orson Welles playing the title role in *The Shadow*. The long running radio crime series ends on 26 December.

Denzil Washington is born on 28 December.

Monday 20: The novelist James Hilton (*Goodbye, Mr Chips*) dies aged 54.

Tuesday 21: The tennis player Chris Evert is born in Fort Lauderdale, Florida.

Wednesday 22: Maxene Andrews of the Andrews Sisters singing group is admitted to hospital after taking an overdose of sleeping pills; her family claim it is an accident.

The US state of Mississippi votes for the right to abolish its public (state) schools if racial desegregation is made compulsory by the federal government.

Thursday 23: The world's first successful kidney transplant is performed by J Hartwell Harrison and Joseph Murray in Boston, Massachusetts.

The Finger of Suspicion by Dickie Valentine and the Stargazers hits number one in the UK singles charts.

Friday 24: Severe storms batter northern Europe; the Belgian freighter *Henri Deweert* goes down with 19 hands off the coast of Texel, Netherlands.

Saturday 25: 28 die when a BOAC Boeing Stratocruiser crashes at Glasgow Prestwick airport.

Sunday 26: The Cleveland Browns win the 1954 NFL American football championships.

The final episode of the crime series *The Shadow* is broadcast, after a 26-year run on US radio.

December 1954

Monday 27: The Vatican orders British Roman Catholics not to join ecumenical organisation The Council of Christians and Jews.

Tuesday 28: The French government votes to allow West Germany to join NATO.

The actor Denzil Washington is born in Mount Vernon, New York.

Wednesday 29: The United States beats Australia in Sydney in the final of the Davis Cup tennis championships.

Britain's first animated feature film, *Animal Farm,* based on the novel by George Orwell, is released.

Thursday 30: The musical *House of Flowers* by Harold Arlen and Truman Capote opens on Broadway.

Friday 31: The mineral Benstonite is discovered, in Magnet Cove, Arkansas.

Tennis player Vic Seixas helps win the Davis Cup for the USA on 29 December.

More titles from Montpelier Publishing

A Little Book of Limericks:
Funny Rhymes for all the Family
ISBN 9781511524124

Scottish Jokes: A Wee Book of
Clean Caledonian Chuckles
ISBN 9781495297366

The Old Fashioned Joke Book:
Gags and Funny Stories
ISBN 9781514261989

Non-Religious Funeral Readings:
Philosophy and Poetry for Secular
Services
ISBN 9781500512835

Large Print Jokes: Hundreds of
Gags in Easy-to-Read Type
ISBN 9781517775780

**Spiritual Readings for Funerals
and Memorial Services**
ISBN 9781503379329

Victorian Murder: True Crimes,
Confessions and Executions
ISBN 9781530296194

Large Print Prayers: A Prayer for
Each Day of the Month
ISBN 9781523251476

**A Little Book of Ripping Riddles
and Confounding Conundrums**
ISBN 9781505548136

Vinegar uses: over 150 ways to use
vinegar
ISBN 9781512136623

Large Print Wordsearch:
100 Puzzles in Easy-to-Read Type
ISBN 9781517638894

The Pipe Smoker's Companion
ISBN 9781500441401

The Book of Church Jokes
ISBN 9781507620632

Bar Mitzvah Notebook
ISBN 9781976007781

Jewish Jokes
ISBN 9781514845769

Large Print Address Book
ISBN 9781539820031

How to Cook Without a Kitchen:
Easy, Healthy and Low-Cost Meals
9781515340188

Large Print Birthday Book
ISBN 9781544670720

Retirement Jokes
ISBN 9781519206350

Take my Wife: Hilarious Jokes of
Love and Marriage
ISBN 9781511790956

Welsh Jokes: A Little Book of
Wonderful Welsh Wit
ISBN 9781511612241

1001 Ways to Save Money: Thrifty
Tips for the Fabulously Frugal!
ISBN 9781505432534

Order online from Amazon or from your local bookshop

Printed in Great Britain
by Amazon